NEGOTIATE LIKE A CHAMPION!

SERIES

FOR REAL ESTATE SELLERS

HOW TO SELL YOUR HOME FAST & MAKE AN EXTRA $5,000 - $50,000!

#1
AUTHORITY
ON REAL-ESTATE
NEGOTIATIONS

STEVEN J. FELDEWERT

ISBN-13: 978-1519590008

ISBN-10: 1519590008

Printed in the USA

For information contact:

Steven J. Feldewert

Ph: (314) 956-6292

E-Mail: Investing@Charter.net

Please visit our website at www.AmericanLandmarkRealty.com

About the Author

Over the past 20+ years, Steven J. Feldewert has been a successful real estate agent, broker, loan officer, developer, and investor. Steve began taking flying lessons in 1984 while initially attending Southwest Missouri State University. He quickly earned his commercial pilot license and flight instructor certification while finishing his degree in Aeronautical Science at Central Missouri State University. He then went on to fly for a regional airline as a co-pilot, captain, and instructor. In 1990, Steve was hired by United Parcel Service as a pilot when he was only 25. While flying, he earned his series 6 and 63 securities licenses, life & health insurance licenses and began buying and selling homes.

In 1996 Steve left United Parcel Service to pursue a full-time career in real estate. He has purchased over 300 residential and commercial properties in the past 20 years, and has presented more than 5,000 offers for himself and his clients. He specializes in negotiations and marketing, and is the only Master Certified Negotiation Expert in the State of Missouri.

Steve's expertise in negotiations has coined him the name "The Negotiator" – He is called on by home buyers, sellers and investors whenever someone wants to absolutely ensure they get the best deal possible on the purchase or sale of a property. Steve is currently the owner and broker of American Landmark Realty which represents buyers and sellers in real estate transactions throughout Missouri. Steve can be contacted by phone or E-Mail for real estate brokerage services, joint-ventures, or for assistance in negotiating any real estate offers. Steve and his wife Sallie live in St. Charles Missouri. Steve can be reached at: (314) 956-6292 or

by E-Mail at: Investing@Charter.net or through his
website: www.AmericanLandmarkRealty.com

Acknowledgments

This book could never have been written without the help, influence, and inspiration of many people. My thoughts, ideas and successes have been formulated over many years. Countless people have contributed and deserve my deep appreciation and gratitude. It will be difficult to name everyone, as that would take several books alone. Sincere thanks go out first and foremost to my wife Sallie who has the toughest job of all….putting up with me on a regular basis! – Without her patience, understanding, sense of humor, and a good deal of tolerance, this book would never have gotten started.

I would also like to thank my daughters Ashlie and Breanna, as without them early on, I wouldn't have had a true reason to persevere.

I would like to express sincere gratitude for my parents who are now deceased. They always put me first in their lives and were the epitome of "givers" especially to me. I miss them dearly.

I would like to thank many of the others who contributed massively to my education and personal development: Anthony Robbins, James Malinchak, Davy Tyburski, Dave Lindahl, Jay Abraham, Dan Kennedy, Bill Glazer, Matthew Ferry, Tom Ferry, Charles Givens, Robert Allen, Stephen Covey, Paul Zane Pilzer, AD Kessler, Dr. Jeffery Lant, Dr. Wayne Dyer, Scott Rister, William Bronchick, Dr. Richard Bandler, Claude Diamond & everyone at the Real Estate Negotiation Institute.

In addition, I'd like to thank the remaining 1,000+ authors and instructors who contributed to my knowledge and education over the years!

I'd also like to thank the rest of my family, friends, and numerous clients over the years. Without them, I wouldn't have a business!

Table of Contents

Introduction

This is how I came to write this book....

I grew up on a small farm in Wentzville Missouri, which is a somewhat small town outside of St. Louis. I thoroughly loved living in the country and the rural life in general, but always strived for new experiences and things to do, see and enjoy. Not overly motivated from a curricular standpoint, I still loved learning. If the material was something I enjoyed, and the subject matter met my criteria for "interesting", I would put 110% of myself into reading, learning, and ingesting every possible bit of information on that subject. For the majority of my school related subjects however this was definitely <u>not</u> the case. Let's just say I "got-by" on the bare minimums, as I'm sure my past instructors and teachers would testify to.

While growing up, my parents always told me that I could get A's <u>if</u> I wanted to. By acknowledging that, they were pretty much letting me know that they knew I was screwing around in school, and not studying enough to pull off A's. I guess hearing that over and over while growing up eventually got me to thinking it was possibly true. Even at that early stage of my life, I pretty much believed I could make, do, or be whatever I wanted. The big question at the time was: "What do I actually want to do?" So, after almost two years of applying myself 110% to the art of partying at College, I ran in to a fellow classmate who was taking flying lessons. At the time, this sounded extremely interesting despite me knowing very little about it from a career standpoint.

Both of my parents originally worked for Ozark Airlines, so I had been exposed to flying as a passenger on many occasions. I remember, even as a young child, thinking it would be cool to be a pilot. Unfortunately, due to some outdated information, I was told you needed to have a military background in order to become an airline pilot. With that erroneous information stuck in the back of my head, I had written off the possibility of flying as a career early on. Fortunately for me, my college buddy was taking flying lessons, and I knew for sure if he could do it, I definitely could too! So, after a brief conversation with him I walked over to the student bookstore and purchased the private pilot manual which was used for the school-taught private pilot ground-school. I hadn't even signed up for this class yet, but figured I'd get started on learning all I could as soon as possible. Once I began reading the book, I now had something exciting that I could turn my passion towards. I remember this year in my life as if it were yesterday. I literally read every book and studied everything I could get my hands on regarding flying and acquiring my pilot's license. Within a week I had made a trip to the airport and quickly secured a flight instructor at Springfield Regional Airport in Springfield Missouri. The first aircraft I flew and later soloed was a Piper Warrior PA-28-151 (see picture on page 4) I began flying daily, and within a few months got my private pilot's license. While attending college, I continued flying as much as my schedule and finances would allow, and soon followed up with my instrument rating, commercial license, multi-engine ratings and flight instructor certificate. I was building flight time as fast as I could, and now had an official career goal of becoming an airline pilot. With that goal in mind, school was no longer a chore, which was reflected in my grades. I went from a 1.9 GPA my first year in college at Southwest Missouri State University to a 3.9 GPA my last year in school at Central Missouri State University.

First Solo Flight in 1984
Piper PA-28-151

In 1987 I graduated from college with a BS degree in Aeronautical Science. I immediately began flight instructing and continuing to build flight time and experience. After approximately 8 months as a flight instructor, and flying every chance that I had, I received my first real opportunity to be hired by an airline. A fellow flight instructor and friend of mine called to let me know he had just gotten hired at one of the regional airlines in St. Louis. After getting off the phone, I put on my suit and tie and promptly went down to their hiring office at Lambert Airport in St. Louis with my logbooks and resume in hand. Fortunately they had an opening in the class and simulator, and after a half hour or so of selling myself, I was also given a job!

In January of 1988, less than one year after graduating college, I was officially hired by a regional airline by the name of Resort Air. (Later named Trans States Airlines) They operated a fleet of nineteen passenger turbo-prop aircraft throughout the Midwest. They later operated under the TWA logo as Trans World Express. (See picture below)

Captain on the Fairchild Swearingen SA-227 (Metroliner)

I was now flying for a regional airline as a co-pilot throughout the Midwest, and having a lot of fun doing it. Shortly after my 24th birthday and within approximately one year of flying as a co-pilot I upgraded to a captain and instructor for the airline. I especially enjoyed flight instructing for the airline which included both the aircraft and the simulator. I had been a flight instructor on small aircraft for a while at this point and teaching something that I loved and enjoyed on a larger aircraft was even better!

Despite loving my job at that time in my life, I still viewed flying for a regional carrier as a stepping stone for my ultimate goal of being hired by a major airline. Major airlines offered better pay, benefits, larger equipment, better schedules and the opportunity to fly to exotic locations. At the time, this sounded like the pinnacle of the profession, and obviously my new career goal.

During this time, many of my peers said they were "attempting" to secure a job with a major airline. I would always ask them: "How many resumes have you sent out?" – "How many interviews have you gone on?" etc…etc…The answer was usually: "None" and "None"

I could not get over how someone who supposedly wanted something that much, yet did absolutely nothing to make it happen. Conversely, in my attempt to get hired, I was sending out resumes by the boxes weekly. I knew I definitely wasn't going to get hired by an airline without at least attempting to market myself. There were many weeks when I would send out 200-300 resumes, turn around and send another 200-300 the next week to the same companies. I was also talking to everyone I could about the job I planned on eventually getting. I asked for referrals, wrote letters, and did everything I could to make my dream job of becoming a major airline pilot happen.

In less than three years from the time I was initially hired by Resort Air, and one year after becoming a captain and instructor with the airline, I was hired by United Parcel Service as a pilot. Being only 25 at the time, I was one of the youngest persons hired at the airline. I was initially trained on the DC-8. (See picture on page 9) I stayed on that airplane the entire duration of my employment. The DC-8 serviced both National and International flying, which allowed me a lot of flexibility in regards to my flight schedule. I enjoyed flying the DC-8 and traveled throughout the world to Europe and Asia. My last several years flying I spent the majority of my time flying between California and

Honolulu, as the tropical environment was definitely my favorite. With great pay, great benefits, and a wonderful schedule (only working about 10 days per month) this was a dream job to most everyone in the airline industry. Despite this being a great job, I still found myself looking for new challenges, and was very much being drawn towards a business of some kind. Having and running a business for some reason appealed to my desire of freedom, unlimited income, and creativity. Little did I know at the time that running a business the wrong way can pretty much eliminate any and all chances of freedom, unlimited income, and creativity!

Piloting the DC-8 for UPS

During this time in my life, I had also become the father of two adorable girls....Ashlie and Breanna. About that same time, I also became the <u>single</u> father of the same two adorable girls. Being out of town for a week or more on a trip with two little girls at home was my idea of emotional torture. Fortunately, during this time I had my Mother who took care of the kids while I was away. She was at a point in her life where she needed someone to need her. Boy did she get her wish! Despite the emotional turmoil, I continued to work and fly for UPS.

My once challenging pilot job had now become just another regular job requiring me to be somewhere I'd rather not be. Flying airplanes throughout the world was exciting, but I was still looking for something more that I could utilize my creativity and desire for business success, and ultimately create some freedom in my life, which I desired even more now that I had two little girls at home. (See picture below)

Daughters Ashlie & Breanna
"My reason for wanting freedom"

At this time in my life, I definitely wanted something more. I began dabbling in other fields attempting to find something I enjoyed that would ultimately provide the freedom and unlimited income I desired. While flying, I got my series 6 and 63 securities license and insurance license. I read everything I could get my hands on regarding finance, money and investing. This was a great learning experience, although cold calling people day in and day out attempting to sell them insurance, annuities & mutual funds was not my ideal job either.

During this time, I had also acquired and studied several real estate courses and in July of 1993 began purchasing distressed single family homes. Most of these homes were foreclosures, pre-foreclosures, REO's and other homes needing extensive repairs and renovations. By 1996 I had purchased, rehabbed, rented and sold over 20 houses. With this experience under my belt, I knew that I could likely support myself and my family with this new found occupation.

So, after almost 6 years of flying for UPS, I put in my resignation. Quitting flying as a career was not an easy task however. I had taken a leave of absence initially, as I could not pull the plug all at once on my piloting career. My whole identity at this time revolved around being a pilot. I remember being physically ill for some time prior to putting in my final resignation. Remember, this was the pinnacle of flying jobs, and by giving up my seniority and leaving this job, I would forever be

11

labeled as "crazy" from my flying peers. Regardless of the future stigma, I pulled the plug on that career in 1996 and began to put everything into growing my business in real estate.

At the time, the real estate market was great, and year after year, we continued to purchase homes. We purchased some to rent out, some to lease with an option to purchase, some to owner finance, and some to immediately resell. – We also began to purchase some commercial properties along with breaking ground on several land development projects. Over the course of 15 years we purchased over 300 properties and built several from the ground up. We also opened a mortgage company, real-estate brokerage business, contracting company, travel business, and handled thousands of transactions overall.

Business at the time was good, although looking back, there were many tell-tail signs of instability. We were making money despite of ourselves. The economy was booming, real estate values were increasing rapidly, and the general outlook of the future was bright. Land values were rising rapidly, and everything looked like it would never end.

Unknowingly at the time however, my business model had one huge significant flaw: I was trying to be the be-all, end-all, do-all for everybody in every situation. I rationalized my decision with the fact all of the businesses were somewhat tied together and related....A real estate brokerage business, a mortgage business, a home renovation business, a contracting business, etc....All of these businesses supported one another, yet what I was actually doing was using one to make up for the lack in the other. Diversifying however, seemed like a rational and sensible choice at the time.

Unfortunately having multiple businesses, employees, and a growing list of responsibilities did not allow me the laser-like focus I needed to put towards one particular specialty and perfect it to the point it literally ran itself. I unknowingly was doing a huge disservice to myself, my employees, and my clients.

Fortunately, (which it didn't seem like at the time) the collapse of the economy and real estate market in 2008 forced me (out of necessity) to totally reorganize, restructure, and regenerate my business.

Initially, this was not without a huge amount of pain, heartache, struggle, and stress both financially, physically, and especially mentally. (I was evidently not a big fan of change, especially when it was forced upon me unwillingly) – This was by far the most painful and stressful time in my life. To add to the stress and heartache, I also lost both of my parents to cancer during this time.

In addition to these stresses, I was also feeling like a complete failure and that I had let down everyone in my life including myself. My family had always supported me throughout my life and business. The thought of letting them down and possibly losing everything I had worked for seemed like the end of the world to me. There were times when I was almost certain I would not survive all of this. Looking back at this, I am actually still amazed that I did survive with the amount of stress I was dealing with daily. I guess there is something to say for human resiliency. Fortunately, the saying "what doesn't kill you makes you stronger" actually worked in my case. I found that each and every day that I "survived" was another day closer to things getting better. I picked out small tasks that needed to be done and began working on them. This also benefited me by taking my mind off the stresses of the business & finances.

This reorganization process took a lot longer than it should have, but slowly and surely I picked up the pieces of a failed business model and began looking at the future with a renewed sense of assurance. At the time, I found myself asking several questions:

1. What do I enjoy doing?
2. What am I good at doing?
3. How can I use this?
4. How can I help serve others massively with this?

These were just a few of the many questions I asked myself, but these four helped me create a new business model and niche for myself.

During my real estate career I had always enjoyed the thrill of negotiating a wonderful deal. I had spent a huge amount of time learning, practicing, and perfecting this area of my business, yet had been diluting my activities with all of the other things that I thought needed to be handled by me. Prior to 2008, I was bidding jobs, managing properties, handling book-keeping, dealing with the normal day-to-day activities that totally took away from what I enjoyed most and what ultimately brought in the majority of income for our business. It was now time for some massive "Change"!

The other area of expertise I had was in marketing. I understood very early on the value of intelligent marketing. Between 1987 and 2007 I had also devoured everything I could get my hands on in regards to creating massive results from marketing and promotion. My first marketing mentor was Jay Abraham. He was introduced to me initially by listening to a Tony Robbins Power Talk program. The Power Talk Series was basically Tony interviewing the best of the best in different areas of business and personal development. Jay Abraham was the marketing genius he was interviewing and the person that went on to teach me much of what I now know about marketing. I consumed everything I could of his, and to this day have his manuals, courses and CD's on my desk as a refresher. Another marketing expert that contributed to my success in sales at the time was Dan Kennedy. Dan has been around for a long time and is considered a marketing "guru." He is also someone I have a huge amount of respect and admiration for and continue to use his strategies in my business.

Most recently at a real estate seminar in Austin Texas, I met James Malinchak. James was on the TV show The Secret Millionaire. He's a well-known public speaker and entrepreneur. James has since mentored me in both marketing and business, and I continue to utilize his expertise in home sales and the promotion of my day-to-day business.

Looking at the past and what I had done initially to succeed led me back to the basics. I had a huge resource of books, tapes, and courses that I hadn't cracked open in quite a while. It was time to get them out, get to work, re-focus, and create a specific niche business that I would enjoy, and would serve my customers and clients massively. Since I had already answered these four questions: What do I enjoy doing? What am I good at doing? How can I use this? How can I help serve others massively with this? - Now I just needed to set in place a great business plan that allowed me to do what I loved and that gave me the freedom I desired.

Realizing that it would be horribly inefficient to reinvent the wheel when it comes to business strategies, I began taking in additional courses, seminars, and speaking to other successful entrepreneurs.
Since I had already determined which part of the business I enjoyed most. – Negotiating (which had no real limits other than those that were self-inflicted) I began organizing ways to expand, grow and perfect this niche.
Prior to even realizing that negotiating was my true "niche" I had found myself working with sellers, and on numerous occasions acquiring properties tens of thousands of dollars below what others had previously

offered. At the time, this excited me, but it also made me curious; and this curiosity led me to research why I was able to pull this off, when many others obviously weren't. This ultimately led me to learn how negotiations really work, and how to capitalize on those strategies.

Working the deals and negotiating was the thing I was looking for. It offered lots of flexibility, and each deal was different. It allowed me the freedom in my business, as I could negotiate great deals on single family homes, commercial real estate, for myself, others, or whatever area I wanted. It allowed me the opportunity to build numerous relationships and some great friendships. With this final determination, I poured my heart and soul into learning and perfecting the art of negotiating. I attended numerous negotiation classes, courses, and trainings, and ultimately became the only Master Certified Negotiation Expert in the State of Missouri.

Today, I no longer see what I do as "a job" but rather my passion! I recently saw a Facebook post that sums this up:

WORKING HARD
FOR SOMETHING
WE DON'T CARE ABOUT
IS CALLED STRESS.
WORKING HARD
FOR SOMETHING
WE LOVE IS
CALLED PASSION.

Chapter One – Can You Really Sell Your Home Fast And Make An Extra $5,000-$50,000?

The quick answer to that question is a resounding "YES!" – I have personally sold hundreds of homes that I owned personally, and thousands for my clients. Depending on the overall price-point of the house, making an extra $5,000 can be as simple as sprucing up the house and implementing a few marketing strategies to get a few more buyers looking at the home. On the higher priced homes, and extra $50,000 or more can also easily be achieved. I see people daily wasting $5,000-$50,000 by not utilizing the strategies outlined in this book. It continues to amaze me that reasonably intelligent people go to great lengths to save $50-$100 on something, yet fail to follow through on some very simple strategies that ultimately would mean and extra $10,000 in their pocket! I guess the term "Penny Wise" and "Pound Foolish" really applies. Don't be that person! Read this book thoroughly, take notes, develop a plan, and follow through! Think how hard you work for $5,000-$50,000 at your job. You can literally make or save an amount equal to a year's salary just by being intelligent and following the simple guidelines provided in this book.

Over the years I have personally purchased over 300 homes with the intention of fixing them up and reselling them for a profit. I made a lot of mistakes during that time, and fortunately have learned from my mistakes. One of the biggest difficulty's I found was determining where to stop in the renovation. Usually the homes I was purchasing were in horrible disrepair, so a gut rehab was in order....These were a "no-brainer" as everything had to be gutted. The houses that were the most difficult were the ones needing minimal updates...It's just harder to determine where to stop. Once one area is updated, painted, and repaired, the remaining areas stand out more as not being updated, painted or repaired....Remember to do what makes sense, yet don't over-improve. Only do repairs that you can get 100% or more of your money back on!

I have written several other books for my Negotiate-Like a Champion series. One is called "How to Make an Extra $5,000-$50,000 when buying a Home." Many of the strategies in this book revolve around finding property where the sellers don't adhere to the suggestions in this book! Someone that doesn't go to the extra effort to prepare their place for sale, who doesn't secure a sales professional who knows how to negotiate effectively, etc...I can literally go out any day of the week, and find a property where I can negotiate a deal which is $5,000-$50,000 below true market value! When selling your home or investment property, don't be the person that "throws away" $5,000-$50,000 just because you failed to follow this advice. Continue reading, as the following chapters will guide you through the steps needed to maximize your profits and ultimate return on your investment.

Chapter Two – Do Your Homework!

This is where I see a lot of people fail when it comes to selling their home. The majority of those who secure my services to market and sell their home have a set dollar amount they'd "like" to get when they sell their home. Most often their pricing rationale revolves around what they owe, what they previously paid, or their emotions in general. Not to discount those issues, as they do play a big part on what someone can, or is, willing to sell their home for. The key when selling a home, however, is to price it within the "sweet spot" based on the market at that specific point in time. Recent sales, current listings, and new inventory can change daily, and therefore have a huge impact on the ability to sell your home at a specific price.

Prior to listing a client's home, I provide a comparative market analysis which is a detailed report of all the similar homes that have sold, expired, and are currently on the market. My goal is to educate a seller, allowing them to see and understand the rationale for my pricing recommendations. When I list a home for a client, I want them to understand "why" I'm doing what I'm doing. I believe an educated seller is much better off than someone who just goes with the flow, blindly trusting someone else. Lots of people got burned with this philosophy during the downturn in the economy and the many Ponzi schemes. Ignorance and greed has been the downfall of many people over the years. Don't let that happen to you! – Expect the best, but plan for the worst! The last thing I want to do is have someone list their home with me only to help sell the neighboring homes that are listed for sale! – This is what happens when a house is over-priced when initially put on the market.

To truly do your homework, you need to size up your competition. You need to find out what other properties are selling for. You need to know what the interiors of your competition looks like. You need to know the average time on the market for your area. You need to know anything and everything about selling your home in order to make an educated decision. Much of this preparation is noted in the upcoming chapter on negotiations. Regardless if you hire someone to sell your home, or sell it yourself, you need to at least do some basic homework and understand the pricing rationale.

Today, on television, (If you have cable) there are many shows (HGTV especially) that show people rehabbing homes for profit. Lots of this information can be extremely beneficial to someone wanting to understand how to prep your home for sale, or the reverse when buying. Just bear in mind, many of these episodes are being filmed in other areas of the country where overall pricing is much different than in the Midwest. If you own a $150,000 home, don't plan on spending $80,000 updating and remodeling your kitchen and expect to make money from it! – In fact, don't even think about getting a small percentage of that money back!

Another area to do your homework in is when hiring help. When you hire a contractor, get references, check out their other work, check them out with the Better Business Bureau, Angie's List, etc….Classic example….This happened to me within the past couple of years. I had a house needing a new roof. I secured the name of a roofer from another real estate agent who has been in the business for a long time and had used this roofer many, many times over the years. She had shared his name and recommended him highly. I had even called and spoke to him a few months before regarding another roof he had looked at for me. I called him and gave him the address of the property needing the roof. He went out their promptly, called me with a price, and indicated he could have it replaced over the weekend. This was late on Thursday. He just needed the $1,500 for materials up front and he'd have it done by late Sunday. Since he was highly recommended, and I trusted him at this point, I went over while he was working on another roof in my neighborhood, and handed him the check for $1,500. Needless to say, the check got cashed, and no work was ever done. He literally vanished! – Despite calls, letters, etc…he was gone! – After some time, I went on to Angie's List and saw that he had recently done this to numerous customers. It appears, despite him being in the business for 20+ years, the downturn in the economy got the best of him. Not that his actions were validated, but if he would have called me and just said: "Hey things are tight, can I take care of another roof down the road for you, etc…" I could have accepted that. Unfortunately for him, he just vanished and quit accepting calls. He has pretty much eliminated the chance of ever getting another roof job in this area. – Bottom line…Do your homework when it comes to everything! Hiring professionals is fine, but a little due diligence will go a long way and keep you out of trouble! Also, get multiple bids, get a signed contract and don't pay for work until it's done!

Another area of "homework" you need to take into account prior to putting your home on the market (primarily if you are selling an investment property that is not your primary residence) is any possible tax implications from the eventual sale. If you've owned the property for a while and have depreciated it during this time, or you are making a sizable profit on the sale you could incur a significant tax liability. This should definitely not be overlooked and hopefully you took this into account long before you decided to sell. This potential "tax hit" can likely be avoided through the use of a 1031 Exchange. Back when I was holding a large portfolio of properties, utilizing a 1031 Exchange saved me tens of thousands of dollars on every property sold. A 1031 Exchange gets its name from Section 1031 of the Internal Revenue Code. As it relates to real property, IRS Section 1031 allows sellers of business or investment property to delay paying capital gains on the sale of this real estate as long as the rules are followed. Here is a brief overview of the rules:

1. Both the property being sold and the "new" property being purchased must be held for investment or business use. Most tax professionals agree that holding the investment or business property for at least one year qualifies the property as an "investment" as opposed to a "fix & flip" property which is held for a shorter time period and is therefore exempt from utilizing a 1031 Exchange.
2. From the day that you sell the property, you have 45 calendar days to identify your replacement property.

3. From the date that you close on the sale of your property you have (180) days to close on your replacement property.
4. The IRS requires that you personally do not touch the funds from the sale of your property. In order to accomplish this, you must utilize a third party called a Qualified Intermediary to facilitate the holding and transferring of funds from the sale.
5. Whatever name title was being held in on the original property, it must match exactly on the replacement property.
6. In order to defer <u>all</u> of the capital gains from a sale, you must purchase a property of equal or greater value and reinvest all of the cash proceeds from the sale.

This is only an overview of the 1031 Exchange process, but basically it allows you to roll the profit from one property to another without being taxed in the year of the sale. This strategy often allows you to save thousands of dollars on each transaction, and the compounding of this savings over time can lead to an even greater savings. I highly recommend you consult a tax professional or attorney that is familiar with exchanges and your specific tax situation prior to proceeding with this strategy.

Chapter Three – Prepare Your Home For Sale!

Remember to think like a buyer when preparing your home for sale! Get everything done before your home is put on the market! This is an area I could also write a book in itself about! It is very difficult to cover all items specifically regarding what may or may not need to be handled prior to putting your home on the market. Regardless, I will list most of the important items:

- Exterior – Make sure the landscaping is neat and orderly. Add mulch if needed. Ensure the lawn is neatly mowed, raked and edged. Trim any trees or shrubs as needed, plant flowers around walk ways and flowerbeds.
- Also clean the outside of the house, spray or power-wash as needed. A quick coat of paint if needed.
- Interior – De-clutter! Put anything you can into temporary storage if necessary. This ultimately makes your home look bigger, allows the prospective buyer to imagine their own items in the home. Also take this time to organize cabinets and closets. Most buyers open both cabinet doors and closet doors. Having less items makes the space look larger and more inviting to a buyer

- Clean, clean, clean! – Anything you can do to make the house spotless will ultimately increase the marketability. Much like a car dealer having a car detailed, the time and money is more than worth the cost to get your home sold fast and for top dollar.
- Smoking….This is a tough one as the majority of buyers are totally turned off by the smell of cigarette smoke. It is also quite difficult to remove the odors and stains caused by the cigarette smoke. Whatever you can do in order to remove the odors, and discontinue smoking in the house will be much benefited.
- Replace worn or defecting flooring. Replacing any badly worn or brightly colored flooring with inexpensive, neutral colored flooring will help tremendously in the sale of your home.
- Consider painting walls, front door, trim, etc….Remember to use neutral colors and have it done professionally. Not to say you can't do it yourself, just make sure it's done neatly and looks good when you're done.
- Change light bulbs as needed. Replace any burned out bulbs and install higher wattages to make your home lighter and brighter.
- Consider professional staging or at least a staging consultation.

The overall goal is to present a clean, spacious, clutter-free home – the kind you'd like to buy! Do a little each day and it will pay dividends! The following is the checklist I provide to my clients when listing their home:

American Landmark Realty's
Home Sale Checklist

Curb Appeal
o Mow lawn
o Trim shrubs
o Edge gardens and walkways
o Weed and mulch
o Sweep walkways and driveways, remove branches, litter and toys
o Add color and fill bare spots with plantings
o Remove mildew or moss from walls or walks with bleach and water
o Take stains off your driveway with cleaner or kitty litter
o Stack woodpile neatly
o Clean and repair patio and deck areas
o Remove any outdoor furniture which is not in good shape
o Make sure pool or spa sparkles
o Replace old storm doors

- Check for flat-fitting roof shingles
- Repair broken windows/shutters, replace torn screens, make sure frames and seams have solid caulking
- Hose off exterior wood and trim, replace damaged bricks or wood
- Touch up exterior paint, repair gutters and eaves
- Clean and remove rust from any window A/C units or store them away
- Paint the front door and mailbox
- Add a new front door mat and consider seasonal door decoration
- Shine brass hardware on front door, exterior lighting fixtures, etc.
- Make sure doorbell is in good working order

General Interior Tips
- Add a fresh coat of interior paint in light neutral colors
- Shampoo carpeting, replace if necessary
- Clean and wax hardwood floors, refinish if necessary
- Clean and wash kitchen and bathroom floors
- Wash all windows, vacuum blinds, wash window sills
- Clean the fireplace

- Clean out and organize closets, add extra space by packing clothes and items you won't need again until after you've moved
- Remove extra furniture, worn rugs and items you don't use: keep papers, toys, etc. picked up, especially on stairs
- Repair easy fixes: loose doorknobs, cracked molding, leaky taps and toilets, squeaky doors, closet or screen doors off their tracks, etc.
- Add dished potpourri or drop of vanilla or bath oil on light bulbs for scent
- Secure jewelry, cash or other valuables

Living Room
- Make it cozy and inviting, discard chipped or worn furniture and frayed or worn rugs
- Consider packing away personal photos
- Remove as much clutter as possible

Dining Room
- Polish any visible silver or crystal
- Set the table for a formal dinner to help viewers imagine entertaining here

Kitchen
- Make sure appliances are spotless inside and out (try baking soda for cleaning Formica stains).

- Make sure all appliances are in perfect working order
- Clean often forgotten spots on top of fridge and under sink
- Wax or sponge floors to brilliant shine, clean baseboards
- Organize item inside cabinets, pre-pack anything you won't be using before your move
- Keep counters as clear and empty as possible

Bathrooms
- Remove all rust and mildew
- Make sure tile, fixtures, shower doors, are immaculate and shining
- Make sure all fixtures are in good shape and lighting is bright, but soft
- Replace loose caulking or grout

Master Bedroom
- Organize furniture to create a spacious look with well-defined sitting, sleeping and dressing areas
- Organize and minimize walk-in closet

Basement
- Sell, give away or throw out unnecessary items
- Organize and create more space by hanging tools and placing items on shelves

- Clean water heater and drain sediment
- Change furnace filter
- Make inspection access easy
- Clean and paint concrete floors and walls
- Provide strong overhead lighting

Attic
- Tidy up by discarding or pre-packing
- Make sure exposed insulation is visible and in good condition
- Make sure air vent is in good working order
- Provide strong overhead lighting

When it's Time to Show
- Make sure all marketing materials are readily available
- Open all draperies and shades, turn on all lights
- Pick up toys and other clutter, check to make sure beds are made and clothes are put away
- Give the carpets a quick vacuuming
- Add some strategically placed fresh flowers
- Open bathroom window for fresh air
- Pop a spicy desert or just a pan of cinnamon in the oven for aroma
- Turn off the TV and put on some light non-offensive music at low volume
- Make a fire in the fireplace (seasonal)

- Put pets in the backyard or arrange for a friend to keep them
- Make sure pet areas are clean and 100% odor-free
- Make sure all trash is disposed

Be careful prior to completing major remodeling projects or additions as you will not normally recoup the cost. Even adding a bathroom, only recoups about 72% of the cost of the addition. Most major remodeling projects to include additions, kitchens, windows, etc…only recoup between 55-70% of the cost. Now if your home is in horrible disrepair anyway, you will obviously recoup much more of this remodeling cost. The average home however, that is moderately outdated, can be cosmetically corrected and you will not only recoup 100+% of the updates, but you will get your home sold quicker.

Another option if you are unsure of your homes overall condition is to have your home inspected by an ASHI certified building inspector prior to putting it on the market. The end buyer will likely have an inspection completed, so you're better off finding out up front what will likely be an issue down the road, and possibly kill the deal before you can correct it. This also allows for time to get bids on repairs and hopefully secure the best pricing. This report will allow you the opportunity to price the home more realistically and be sure of it. This extra step if handled properly will show your buyer you are up front and honest, and willing to handle things as needed. This building inspection if used in the marketing can substantiate a higher asking price up front and demand a higher negotiated price, knowing all potential issues are handled. Once the building inspection is handled, make all necessary repairs and include paid invoices to the new prospective buyers. Also, provide a copy of the survey if you have one.

Another recommendation if you have doubts on value is to have your home professionally appraised. I generally discourage my clients from spending the $300-$400 for this as I have access to, and provide the same information the appraisers use in formulating an appraisal. I sometimes wish my clients would get an appraisal however, as quite often they have a preconceived idea what their house is worth with nothing to back it up, other than an irrational emotionally biased opinion of value. As I tell them....Neither of us determines the market price of a home. The market is what it is and it alone will regulate what your home ultimately sells for. Even if I could magically hypnotize prospective buyers into writing a contract regardless of price, ultimately when the buyer secures financing and the lenders appraiser shows up, the house will only appraise for what the market shows it should sell for, which ultimately revolves around comparable sales. On numerous occasions between 2008-2011 I have had a buyer excited to purchase at list price only to have the appraiser come in tens of thousands of dollars less, ultimately killing the deal because the home wouldn't appraise. Remember, the market is what the market is!

Most often, I can hedge the offer price with aggressive marketing and negotiations, but all within reason. After the 2008-2011 market crash, most buyers are much more cost conscious and savvy to the market. No one wants to "over pay" and few buyers are willing to pay significantly more than a house is worth after viewing comparable sales and an appraisal!

Chapter Four – Deciding How to Sell Your Home

Selling Your Home Yourself (FSBO)

In 1993 when I first started buying and selling homes, I had the choice of getting my real estate license or not. At the time, it did provide some additional access to homes via the MLS. Since there were definitely some costs involved such as licensing, annual dues, fees, etc....I initially put off getting my license. A few years later, my attorney suggested not getting licensed due to the much higher liability and the fact I only wanted the license to increase my access to homes listed on the MLS. With this being the case, I continued to hold off, which was a good choice, as I was able to buy and sell over 100 houses without this expenditure in time and money.

Between 1993 and 1997, I purchased and sold many houses without the aid of a real estate agent. I did however spend a great deal of money on advertising, which at the time was traditional newspaper advertising. At the peak of our home selling business I was spending around $2,000 per month on these newspaper advertisements. In my area, we utilized the St. Charles Journal, St. Louis Post Dispatch, and occasionally the Thrifty Nickel. Granted we were spending a good deal of money, but I was getting what I considered excellent results. We were selling houses easily and regularly utilizing these methods along with some signs and flyers. – Remember, this was "before" Craigslist, Facebook, E-Bay, Realtor.com, Trulia, Zillow, etc….The main resources for advertising back then was the good old fashioned newspaper!

With much trial & error, and lots of practice I became extremely effective selling our homes without utilizing an agent or broker. I was also very confident I could market and sell a house better than any real estate agent or broker could! Now granted, this was not a casual sale here and there. By this time I had devoted my business, career, and livelihood around buying, improving, marketing, and selling homes. I wasn't just someone working part-time trying to sell one house. This had become my specialty, and by that time I had already hired help. I had a full time crew working on these homes, and a full time assistant who answered calls, distributed flyers, assisted with marketing, etc…

For some reason however, between 1997 and 2000 our traditional newspaper advertising results started dropping off. We were doing the same thing that was effective for the past 7 years, now with very little return. It appeared that the majority of new home buyers were leveraging their time by utilizing a real estate agent to secure a new home. What I once considered a niche business (selling by owner) was now slowly phasing out and costing us time and money. Out of curiosity I did a little survey of my own, and found that approximately 94% of buyers would only call and agent to help them locate and secure a new home when the time came to purchase. Even buyers who had located a FSBO on their own would likely contact an agent to help them with the sale. This little survey proved why we were getting fewer callers and our marketing strategies were no longer working. In addition, the majority of the prospective buyers we were encountering were investors trying to make a buck on what they considered a "wholesale" opportunity just because it was a FSBO. Most of any offers we were now getting were "lowball" from someone trying to get a great deal for resale. This obviously did not work, as we had already purchased at wholesale and were trying to get a retail price. Some additional research revealed that less than 9% of all the homes on the market are being marketed without the use of an agent. Of those homes being marketed as a FSBO, 89% will eventually list with an agent or take their home off the market entirely. The small percentage that do sell, sell for 15% less than homes listed with an agent.

With this newfound knowledge, I put my wife up to the challenge of getting "re-licensed" as she had held her real estate license years before we met. Immediately upon her getting re-licensed and listing our homes, we saw a noticeable improvement in our marketing efforts. Having the properties in the MLS and accessible to the real estate agent community provided a huge difference in our business, and we quit spending the $2,000+ per month on newspaper ads! After several years, I got my real estate license and broker's license, to not only use for investment, but to help others acquire and sell properties as well.

This may seem like a somewhat biased opinion, as I am a full-time real estate broker and own my own real estate brokerage company, but in my professional opinion, I would urge anyone needing to sell a home to obtain help from a competent professional. Selling a home without the assistance of an experienced real estate professional is like representing yourself in court. It can be done, but likely not your best option. For most home sellers, this is not something they are going to do very often, and truthfully, selling a home is a lot of work. If you add up all the hours a real estate agent or broker spends selling a home less their out of pocket expenses such as advertising, marketing, licensing, printing, gas, etc…you'll see they earn considerably less than any other comparable professional. A professional real estate agent will assist with the following:

- Implementing strategies in this book
- Representing you and protecting your interests.
- Providing market information and recent sales statistics.
- Providing, drafting & reviewing contracts.
- Advertising your home on the MLS
- Placing a for sale sign in your yard
- Provide a "take one" box and flyers for your home.
- Placing your home on their company website.
- Placing your home on Craigslist.
- Placing your home on numerous other sites.
- Advertising, marketing & holding an open house.
- Having professional photos of your house taken.
- Providing a SUPRA lockbox allowing tracking of all persons entering your home.
- Providing advice on prepping your home for market.
- Providing staging advice
- Providing a list of "recommended" professionals.
- Providing agent tours of your home.
- Direct marketing to other agents.
- Pre-qualifying prospective buyers.

- Provide assistance to buyer with financing.
- Showing your home (even if you're not home)
- Responding to telephone inquiries on your home.
- Analyzing and negotiating offers.
- Writing and presenting counter-offers.
- Ensuring compliance with fair housing laws.
- Ensuring compliance with disclosure requirements.
- Consulting with attorneys, inspectors, etc…
- Arranging for bids, repairs, and meeting contractors.
- Coordinating utility changes.
- Meeting appraisers & building inspectors.
- Reviewing the title company settlement documents prior to closing
- Attending a walk-thru with buyer.
- Attending and assisting the seller/buyer at closing.

A really good agent will also be a <u>marketing and negotiations expert</u> and recoup several times over the cost for their services. The key is hiring the right agent who specializes in these two areas!

When searching out a company to sell your home, remember - Bigger is not always better!

In searching out someone to represent you in one of the most important financial decisions of your life, remember this! – Bigger is not always better! – When I was starting out, I had dreams of creating a huge company with hundreds of employees, big offices, etc....I am pretty sure this was ego driven on my part, but aside from that, I wanted to be the be-all, do-all, end-all, for everybody and everything. Needless to say I quickly found out I would be doing a huge disservice to my clients, not to mention myself by going this route with my business.

This was even more apparent when I became involved with banks handling short sales and REO's I saw the incredible inefficiencies taking place daily. I had seen banks lose over a hundred thousand dollars in a week, on one house just because one hand didn't know what the other hand was doing. (Despite being told numerous times!) The bigger the banks the worse this seemed to be. This unfortunately applies to most large companies, real estate included. This is not to say you can't find a great agent that works for CBG, RE/MAX, Keller Williams, Berkshire-Hathaway, etc...There are many great agents out there who work for bigger companies and do an excellent job. Just bear in mind they do have policies, procedures, and bureaucracy that can sometime interfere with the simple-act of getting things done.

This doesn't mean you should hire some fly-by-night company or individual either. It basically just means you need to search out a specialist. This applies to almost everything in life: Doctors, Lawyers, Financial Advisors, etc....You should do whatever it takes to ensure you hire a specialist who's successful occupation revolves around a very specific area of expertise. In my life, I've since learned I must search out someone that is the best of the best at what they do if I expect to get the results I desire. Most times it is from a smaller company or individual who has very specialized knowledge and who has literally perfected their services in the area of help I am looking for.

Selecting an Agent

This is a big question many people ask: Who should I hire to sell my home?" Most people hire someone they know, a relative, or someone that was referred to them. When it comes to selling what is likely the largest investment in your life, you need to be sure you are making the right decision. To make this decision even more difficult, there are hundreds of real estate agents, brokers, and companies to pick from. Out of the many agents out there, some sell real estate part-time, others full time. Some have countless designations, others none.....

So How Do You Decide?

When it comes to selling your home, it's obvious you need someone that's a true professional and treats real estate as their main profession as opposed to a part-time hobby. It's also obvious you need someone with a high degree of experience to rely on, and who invests regularly in their education.

These qualities, along with pricing your home correctly (and not over pricing it) are likely what everyone can agree are needed to effectively market and sell one of our most important financial assets – Our home.

So How Do I Pick Then?

When hiring someone to sell your home there are (2) things your real estate agent <u>absolutely</u>, <u>positively</u> must be in order to get your home sold quickly for top dollar….

1 – A Master Marketer!

Hiring a master marketer is by far the most important aspect of getting your home sold! Marketing is the key behind reaching the greatest number of potential buyers, and thus massively increasing the chances of selling your home. Whoever you hire, make sure this is the #1 quality they possess!

2 – A Negotiation Expert!

Hiring an expert in negotiations allows you to increase your bottom line proceeds by thousand, if not tens of thousands of dollars. Few agents possess the real expertise in this area of real estate. Whoever you hire, make sure this is one of the top qualities they possess! And remember…most moderately successful full-time real estate agents have the ability to sell houses, but very, very few are truly masters of marketing and negotiations which is ultimately what allows you to sell your home fast and make and extra $5,000-$50,000!

Chapter Five – "Massive" Marketing!

Regardless of how you sell your house, or who you use to sell it, you or they must market massively! As previously mentioned not all agents know how to effectively market a home, or even themselves for that matter. Most agents put the house in the MLS, throw out a sign and hope for the best. Now granted, once on the MLS there are hundreds if not thousands of other agents who have access to it and the listing flows through to other websites like Realtor.com, Zillow, Trulia, etc…And truthfully, in a seller's market, this allows for the majority of homes to be sold within a reasonable amount of time. It does not however provide the maximum leverage of finding numerous buyers all wanting your home and thereby creating a buyer-frenzy and increasing your net proceeds by $5,000-$50,000 on the sale. This takes massive marketing from either yourself if you are selling "by-owner" or your agent if you have hired one.

Having been trained by some of the best marketing minds in the world (Dan Kennedy, Jay Abraham & James Malinchak) I've learned this is the one area of your business that you can increase your profits geometrically with very little expenditure. You don't need large expensive billboards, TV advertising, etc…to get big results.

As marketing genius Jay Abraham says in his X-Factor course:
1. *People are silently begging to be led.*
2. *People need to be told what specific action to take*
3. *Marketing is the ultimate financial leverage.*
4. *Advertising is nothing more than salesmanship.*
5. *People don't know what you can do for them unless you educate them to the facts.*
6. *Bonuses can make a wonderful contribution to your sales promotion.*
7. *Turn the tables on the risk factor when making a sales proposition*

When selling a house there are numerous methods of effective marketing that gets the house out to the greatest number of people, thus increasing the probability of a securing a buyer quickly and making an additional $5,000 - $50,000! Here are a few we utilize "just" for an open house alone!

- Advertise Open House on MLS
- Advertise Open House on Facebook (personal)

- Advertise Open House on Facebook (business page)
- Advertise Open House on Craigslist
- Advertise Open House on Zillow
- Advertise Open House on Twitter
- Advertise Open House on our website
- Advertise Open House and send mass E-Mails to our database utilizing Constant Contact
- Utilize Open House Yard Sign with Call Capture system.
- Utilize Listing Booster with Call capture and E-Mail capture system.
- Utilize Virtual Tours.
- Utilize Flyers with "call to action"
- Utilize Directional Signs with Balloons.
- Send out direct mail flyers, letters, announcement's promoting the open house.
- Utilize "Every Door Direct" postcards for advertising.
- Utilize Phone Calls to past clients and individuals in our database.
- Utilize agent E-Mail marketing campaign to promote open house.
- Utilize QR codes on signs, flyers and marketing material.

In addition, most of these actions have very specific ways of doing them and another checklist within a checklist to ensure they are being handled and managed in the most efficient and effective way possible. From the color and typeset of the print, the layout of the flyer, the number of photos, color of the balloons.....All of these actions are again broken down, and I ask myself the following question: How can I do this better? – What would increase the marketing effectiveness by even just 1%? – Asking yourself these questions many times over the years, you eventually come up with incremental ideas that after much testing, lead to very effective methods to absolutely, positively, maximize the overall marketing results and thus increase the probability of selling your home for a higher price. Also, by utilizing the expertise and specialized knowledge of marketing professionals such as Jay Abraham, Bill Glazer, Dan Kennedy and James Malinchak, I can further leverage my time and efforts.

Learning the good old fashioned way by trial and error and testing works fine, it just takes longer and costs considerably more. Unfortunately I've spent a great deal of time learning this way too. (The hard way) Fortunately, I can at least now share these experiences with my clients.

Chapter Six – Negotiate Like a Champion!

Every buyer and seller wants to feel like they got a great deal. Unfortunately most buyers and sellers in general haven't a clue how to negotiate effectively. – As many personalities there are out in the world, there are people negotiating by different methods. – Many play hardball and completely beat up the seller, only to have the seller refuse to sell the property even for top dollar. The buyers are thinking they are just being savvy negotiators, but often just eliminate their chances of getting even a remotely good deal. – I cannot tell you how many times I've purchased property for myself, or negotiated for someone else that a previous offer was provided at $10,000-$75,000 more than I ultimately negotiated. What does that tell you about the majority of the population's ability to effectively negotiate?

Regardless of the method that people use, everyone wants to at least "think" they got a good deal. This applies primarily to buyers, but even sellers need to rationalize their ultimate sales price in their head.

In regards to negotiations, I've met a few really good attorneys that specialize in this area, and can work wonders for their clients. Unfortunately, many others that promote themselves as "fighting" for their clients only complicate negotiations. What do you automatically think of when you think of someone "fighting" you? Well, most see it as an attack, and automatically provide resistance against such an attack. Just having an attorney sets the stage for "fighting" and automatically provides resistance against such a move. This is what you see many times in divorces. One person hires an attorney who promises to fight for their clients rights. This move sets the stage for automatic resistance by the other party hiring an attorney to counter the attack and resist that move. – Ultimately the attorney's win out since they are paid by the hour to "fight" for their client. Now I'm not advocating discarding the use of an attorney for certain transactions, I'm only suggesting that you ultimately need to look at what you're trying to accomplish, and if that is to purchase or sell something, there must me collaboration amongst parties, and there are certain ways to go about that which will statistically put you in the driver's seat when beginning these negotiations, and ultimately lead you to a successful outcome.

What few people actually realize, is that buyers and sellers ultimately buy or sell based on emotion and justify based on logic. Persuading other in negotiations ultimately revolves around two motivating forces:

1. Pain (appeal to their fear of loss)
2. Pleasure (appeal to their desire for gain)

Pain & Pleasure are the motivating forces that drive all human activity, and statistically speaking, most humans are primarily motivated by pain (or their fear of loss)

Successfully persuading others in negotiations ultimately revolves around these two motivating forces, but can be broken down further into seven additional categories:

1. Logic: People are persuaded by sound logical reasoning. (providing credible proof in negotiations will help tremendously)
2. Self-Interest: People are persuaded by what is obviously in their best interest. (providing them with proof the outcome of this negotiation will be in their self-interest)
3. Exchange: In business, people have a sense of obligation when exchanging things of value. (since you gave me this – I'll give you that)
4. Sameness: This is a universal connection whereby people like people that are like them.
5. Communication: Communicating effectively revolves around not only spoke words, but tonality, tempo and all other aspects of body

language. All three of these play a very important role in effective communication and ultimately effective negotiation.

6. Uniqueness: People in general desire something more if it is scarce or of limited quantity or time.

7. Contrast: Providing evidence your choice is clearly the better one by magnifying the alternative.

These seven categories of persuasion techniques are the basis of how and why people make their decisions in life and in all negotiations. Understanding this negotiation process will ultimately help you make an additional $5,000-$50,000 on the sale of your home or investment property!

My initial delay in writing this book was due to my desire to write a book with "everything" addressed regarding negotiations. I eventually realized it would take several large books to cover all of the intricacies of the negotiation process. Real estate negotiations have numerous complexities such as buyer, seller & agent attitudes & personalities, differences in communication, pricing, values, commissions, fees, financing, timing, earnest money deposits, closing costs, appraisals, inspections, repairs, legal issues, other offers, marketing, personal property, and a huge range of human emotions.

Since it wasn't practical to include 500 pages on the specifics of negotiations, I elected give you the reader an overview of these negotiation principals and likewise the tools to ultimately make or save $5,000 - $50,000 on your next sale. The following are the 3 steps to effective negotiating:

Step # 1 - Gathering Information

"Negotiation is an information game. Those who know how to obtain information perform better than those who stick with what they know"

Deepak Malhotra
Harvard Law School

The first step in negotiating anything with anyone ultimately revolves around gathering information. Skilled negotiators gather information by asking numerous questions, researching statistics, repeating statements as questions, confirming understanding and questioning third parties.

I see numerous people every-day begin negotiations without ever doing their homework. As former head-coach of the Denver Bronco's Mike Shanahan says in his book:

"Preparation is Key." - Having prepared for every possible contingency. "Break down the competition's weakness and learn from their strength's." – There's a system to studying game films, to observing your competitors on their home field before a big game. Apply it every time you enter a new market, pitch to a new customer, face a critical decision or most importantly prior to beginning any negotiations.

When first starting out in the real estate business, I had developed my own checklist of items that would most benefit me in the upcoming negotiations. This "checklist" mentality originated from my flying career. Everyone that flies airplanes knows that the likelihood of making a mistake is significantly increased when not utilizing a checklist. A good checklist eliminates the possibility of missing something and allows you to focus on the task at hand instead of relying on memory. Write things down and you'll never forget them. Later in my career, I adapted a negotiation planning guide developed by the Real Estate Negotiation Institute. This guide was much better organized and ultimately allows me to come up with a perfect negotiation strategy for each individual deal. This guide has been invaluable in organizing my thoughts and planning.

Prior to starting negotiations on any real estate offer, I find out as much as I can in regards to the interest & needs of the buyer, seller, market data, property data, negotiation styles of who I will be dealing with, negotiation goals, and finally what I will do if we fail to reach an agreement in the current negotiation.

To determine the interest & needs of the buyer or seller, I ask numerous questions. Finding out their needs and wants provides a good degree of leverage before we even begin negotiating. Beginning with a few open-ended questions is typically the best way to start the process. Open-ended questions are questions that cannot be answered with a typical "Yes" or "No" They are designed to explore options and are "Who" "What" "Why" "When" "Where" and "How" questions. Closed-ended questions can be answered with a "Yes" or "No" and speculative questions are designed to encourage vision and possibilities. Following up with some close-ended and speculative questions provides an opportunity to find out what will likely motivate the buyer or seller.

The specific questions you ask will depend on if you are dealing with the seller directly or likely an agent of the seller. Just a few of the possible questions include:

- Is your listing still available?
- Are you still asking $_____ for the property?
- Is this the original price?
- How long has the property been on the market?
- Have you had much interest in the property?
- Do you have any current offers on the property?
- Did you have any previous offers on the property?
- What time frame is the buyer/seller looking for on a closing?
- Is owner-financing "all" or "part of" the sale an option?

In researching the market data, I find out everything I can in regards to sales of other comparable listings. Knowing what properties have sold, the price, condition, and how long they were on the market gives me a distinct advantage when beginning any negotiation. Knowing the general market conditions, comps, CPI/Inflation rate, general economy, unemployment rates, interest rates, number of active listings and absorption rate allow me to have a good understanding of the market. This understanding gives me a distinct advantage in future negotiations. Fortunately, as a real estate broker, I have access to much of this information through the Multiple Listing Service and statistical information I have saved over the years. For others that are not licensed real estate brokers or agents, much of this information can be provided by other real estate professionals, appraisers or through online research. When negotiating, I research every property that is active, sold and pending within a certain geographical area. I want to know not only what the competition is, but the specific condition, number of days on the market and also the general direction the market is heading. This information gives me a huge advantage when negotiating the purchase or sale of a property. It is difficult to argue with "the facts." Strategically using those facts in your negotiation definitely give you a leg up on your competitor.

In researching the property data, I utilize numerous resources depending on the type of property. Much of the information I have access to comes from the MLS, assessor's database, neighbors, past listing or selling agents, etc.. For average residential properties I use my own cursory inspection and note any and all deficiencies. I utilize the use of a camera and notes to ensure I remember any and all deficiencies. I want to know the days on market for this property, and the history of the listing. Knowing about past or current offers, price reductions, improvements, highlights and concerns all help with negotiations in the future. In addition to this, building inspectors will often provide a more thorough inspection and will quite often come in to play after the initial offer is presented. Knowing which deficiencies to present to the seller initially, and which ones to wait on for on the building inspection will help you negotiate more successfully. Asking for something initially, along with other items that will likely be addressed in a building inspection lead the seller to likely reject your request and limit the concessions you will ultimately receive. Don't bother asking for something you'll likely receive anyway, just at a later date.

In addition, I also research everything I can that gives me leverage regarding the building, square footage, current income, past income, tenants, underlying mortgages, price that was paid, when it was initially purchased, who purchased it. I research any and all underlying "issues" such as repairs needed, and any deficiencies. This level of preparation takes some time, but can be leveraged through the use of building inspectors, appraisers, contractors, etc. The time involved in this preparation is directly proportional to the type of building being purchased. – For a single family home, it can be accomplished quite easily through the use of an experienced real estate agent or broker, appraiser and a building inspector, which is what most buyers will opt for anyway. – Upon receiving these documents, they must be analyzed. Creating an outline of all "issues" deficiencies, etc... will serve as leverage for negotiating later down the road.

Larger properties such as multi-family apartment buildings, commercial buildings, and industrial sites require numerous additional "due-diligence" methods to include Phase 1 & Phase 2 Environmental Inspections, City and County reviews, Best Use Analysis, Engineers, Architects, etc.....Lots of homework to say the least. Fortunately there are professionals that provide the knowledge needed for this analysis. The key here is to find "good' professionals that are very specific to your project. Don't hire someone unless they are specialists in their field of expertise, and in the subject you need.

I once hired an engineering company to handle the civil engineering of a residential development project I was working on. This company had been around a long time, was extremely experienced and expensive. This was my first development project, and unknown to me at the time, they specialized in commercial development, as opposed to residential development. They were capable of doing residential, but most of their business revolved around commercial. They in turn demanded higher prices and ultimately cost us over $750,000 in profits. Research not only begins with the property you will be negotiating on, but the individuals you will need to analyze your deal. Referrals are definitely a start, but make sure you complete your own due diligence even after being referred to someone. – Sometimes the best intention of someone isn't always in your best interest. Don't be lazy, due your homework.

One of the next steps in the information-gathering stage is to analyze the competition. Find out everything you can about other properties for sale, that have sold, and the specifics regarding those sales. Also, gathering statistical information regarding past, current, and future market statistics will help you negotiate from a level of power. There should not be a question regarding this property or any of the competition you don't know. This informational gathering process is much like an attorney who is preparing for a case. One little piece of information can make the difference between winning and losing a case, or possibly mean the difference of $1,000 - $100,000 or more in price savings. Is an extra hour or two of research worth at least $1,000 to you? If so, read on......

Utilizing a good appraiser can help or hinder your negotiations. Required on most financed residential and commercial purchases, disclosing the appraised price to the other party is not required unless the appraisal had come in lower and set in motion an appraisal contingency. Bottom line: Use it if it helps you're your negotiating strategy. This "low appraisal" occurrence was quite frequent between 2008 and 2012 when we were seeing approximately 20% of appraisals coming in significantly lower than the contract sales price. Fortunately in the majority of my business as a buyer's agent this happened rarely as I specialize in finding, negotiating, and securing properties for others at significant discounts which are usually significantly below-market price. It was however a big problem with my listings.

Another important thing in gathering information is analyzing your seller, agent, or whoever you will ultimately be negotiating with, and their style of negotiation. You'll need to size up their personality and motivational triggers.

One of the most valuable assets to my negotiating career was learning about, and becoming a Certified Master Practitioner of NLP (Neuro-Linguistic Programming).

A quick definition of NLP is the systematic study of human performance that teaches people how to effectively utilize their brains, change behavior, self-motivates and ultimately strive for excellence. This training taught me valuable tools to connect with others and build rapport. People like people that they think are like themselves. The simple act of mirroring and matching helps you build rapport and connect and communicate better. One of the masters of NLP, Tony Robbins, provided some wonderful insights to the art of NLP. At one of his seminars I attended, I remember him doing an onstage conversation with one of the attendees. The exercise was intended to show the other attendees how mirroring and matching worked. It was amazing how he was able to carry on a conversation with someone he picked out of the audience, begin to mirror her mannerisms and tonality. He was accentuating everything to show his point, but it was still not perceived by her. He normally would have been a little more subtle about how he did this, but it was still not noticeable to this person he was conversing with. To the rest of the group, it was almost humorous how he was able to mirror, match, and eventually lead her exactly where he wanted her to go in the conversation. Now this may sound like manipulation, but the bottom line, it made her ultimately connect with him more, feel more

important, and have a level of rapport beyond what most people could ever do.
Utilizing this technology can benefit you greatly in negotiations.

When analyzing your opponent in the negotiations it is a very good idea to determine their personality types. Some negotiators are competitive (win-lose), others are collaborative (win-win) and others are compliant. (lose-win) Once you have sized up the other party, you need to create of list of items you are willing to give them. This list of items will be a tool you can use later in the negotiations. Many times there are things you can offer that have little importance to you, but have a much greater value for the other party. Asking lots of questions in an attempt to identify the real area of needs and wants provides a distinct advantage down the road.

Buyers primarily, but also sellers make their initial decision emotionally and justify with logic. This method uses both left and right sides of the brain. Everyone has a predominant side of the brain they use, and it's our job as a negotiator to find out what is the most motivating factor to use. Here is where questioning pays off big.

Step # 2 – Determining Options

Now that you've gathered all of the pertinent information, you will need to come up with an ultimate goal or "range" associated with price and or specific terms of the sale. As they say….You can't reach the goal without having a specific target. This "range" should include an aggressive, moderate, and realistic value. Once you've determined your overall negotiation goals, you will need to consider the potential outcomes and how you will respond. You'll need to determine a minimum price you are willing to accept. You will also need to set realistic expectations based on the research you have come up with.

With extensive experience and records of past purchases I can usually determine the price I will pay for a property within 3% with 95% accuracy. I have fortunately kept extensive records on past offers for specific types of properties and specific owners: retail sellers, Fannie Mae foreclosures, Freddie Mac foreclosures, HUD owned foreclosures, short sales, etc. As a buyer, short sales are currently a favorite of mine, and I've been surprised at some of the prices I've been able to negotiate. There are many variables with short sales, but most revolve around the person handling the initial short sale negotiations. Ultimately the final price comes down to an appraisal or BPO (broker price opinion) which is ultimately one person's opinion of value. This "opinion" can vary greatly, but often come out in the buyers favor.

The next step is to analyze and anticipate what the other party will do. Taking time to do this is essential in effective negotiations. Similar to a chess game, the winner most often is the one who analyzes and anticipates the future moves of their opponent the best. You must be able to put yourself in their shoes and anticipate what they will say and how they will respond. Doing this effectively give you a huge edge in your negotiations.

One of the final tasks in determining your options is to determine what you will do and what will happen if you fail to reach an agreement with this negotiation. It is essential you know this before actually entering into a negotiation. You must also make this option look attractive from your stand-point without revealing specifics to your competitor. Some options include:

- Not purchasing now
- Purchasing another property
- Concede to the others terms

Regardless of how the negotiations go, you'll need to have a well thought out plan and determine your options well in advance.

Step # 3 – Developing a Strategy

Upon gathering all of the pertinent information and determining your options, you will then need to develop a sound negotiation strategy. You must also utilize the skills of effective communication, along with identifying values, exploring options, persuading and influencing, building trust, and utilize the skills and tactics of a competitive and collaborative negotiator.

Creating Value in Your Offer

"Negotiating theory teaches, among other things that it is necessary to probe beneath state demands and positions and ask what is actually important to the other side and what do they value"

Robert H. Mnookin
Harvard Law School

One of the first steps prior to presenting an offer or counter-offer is to determine what the other party values most. There are numerous types of value to include:

- Money
- Time
- Relationships
- Fairness
- Contract Specifics
- Reputation
- Cooperation
- Etc...

As mentioned previously in this book, asking open ended questions to gather information from the buyer is most helpful. Some additional questions include:

- How did you arrive at that?
- Why do you think that?
- How would that work?
- How can I better explain that?
- Where did you get that information?
- What will it take to _____?
- Why is that important to you?
- Why do you feel that way?
- What is your primary concern?
- How could we improve this outcome?
- Where is the data to back this up?
- How does this help?

Creating Value involves identifying needs, interest and values first. You must then explore options and alternatives and ultimately build trust. Showing concern and building trust are an important part of any negotiations. The above referenced questions convey to the other party that you are genuinely concerned and their level of trust is increased. Generally speaking, start with a few open-ended questions to get the other party thinking in a certain way, and then switch over to some closed-ended questions to get specifics and build rapport. Throwing in a few speculative questions opens up the thought process and encourages possibilities.

When I initially meet with a buyer or agent, I begin by getting to know them better. I quite often ask numerous questions to get them involved and to develop a good level of rapport prior to asking more probing questions. This usually creates a better environment for future communication and trust building. Building trust up front opens up for more sharing of information, reduces stress, and ultimately improves the relationship between parties which also provides better outcomes for all involved.

I'm still surprised every time I meet someone initially and they are the most stand-offish, closed-minded, and generally "not-nice" person I've ever met, and within 5-

10 minutes of interaction they have warmed up and are as nice as can be.

Chapter Seven – Selling with a "Lease Purchase"

This is an area most sellers either don't understand or they are completely scared to even entertain it as a possibility. Basically this revolves around being creative in the way you structure the sale. One of the ways you can sell a home is through a "Lease Purchase" or "Lease Option".

This method allows a prospective buyer to lock in a price today while leasing until a pre-determined date, whereabouts they will ultimately purchase. Normally the buyer puts down a certain dollar figure allowing them "the right" or "option" to purchase sometime during that time. Over the years I have completed hundreds of these deals personally and have had excellent results. Basically it can be a win-win for both parties, both buyer and seller. During my real estate career, there have been several times when the market slowed. My business success at the time revolved around getting the house sold or at least offsetting the negative cash flow of the monthly payments of principal and interest, not to mention the taxes and insurance. I had usually just purchased the home with cash or the equivalent, put out a large expenditure for repairs and remodeling and now needed an exit plan. With this large outlay of cash, it was quite often difficult or impossible to purchase another home until that property sold. With a slowing market it often put a severe hold on our business growth and limited opportunities when great deals came up. To overcome this obstacle, I began refinancing the property, pulling out all my initial investment and securing a tenant who ultimately wanted to purchase the home. I would then sell the home at a premium price, which was based on a projected value 1-3 years in the future. The length of this term was determined by the length of the time the buyer needed to ultimately secure financing. Offering these terms, (which few others were offering at the time) allowed me to name my price. Most buyers were not that concerned about the final purchase price, but rather what the monthly payments were and if they could afford them. Not that this was the most intelligent decision on their part, but at the time homes were appreciating rapidly, and a house currently worth a maximum of $100,000 as a retail sale, would easily bring $110,000-$125,000 just a year or two later.

To market these homes, I would advertise them as "Rent-To-Own" as most people understood that term. With this strategy, I could easily fill any vacancies fast. In addition, I would ask for a minimum of $3,000 as option consideration. This money was what gave the renters the right to purchase for a predetermined amount of time (generally 1-2 years) – I would also give the tenants incentive by allowing a "rent credit" if the rent was paid on-time each month. This might range from $100-$300 per month that would be applied towards the purchase when the home closed. This "credit" would only apply if and when they purchased. In the event they did not purchase, they would not get this credit back or get a refund on their option money. I set it up this way to ensure my tenant-buyers were serious and did ultimately buy my house. I would also pre-qualify them myself to ensure there was a very good likelihood they could and would ultimately purchase. Statistically, over 94% of my buyers ultimately purchased. Other investors using this strategy had a lower percentage of buyers, but they realized they could just collect additional option money, up the price, and re-rent the unit. I realized I could have made more money this way but felt a moral obligation to do whatever I could do to ensure my buyers could and would perform on the purchase.

This strategy is great in a slow market, but does carry some additional work and risk as the house will have to be rented, and that alone scares most people. In addition, most people selling their own home will need to pay-off their current mortgage in order to purchase another home. This strategy is only pertinent to those having the flexibility and financial capability to qualify for another separate mortgage, or have the cash to purchase a separate home.

Chapter Eight – Selling with "Owner Financing"

Another effective and creative way to sell is to offer owner financing. This can be accomplished by either financing the sale outright or keeping the existing financing in place and selling the home on contract (contract for deed, installment land contract, etc...) Without getting overly complicated, this method involves the seller acting as the bank and getting monthly payments instead of all the money up front. This doesn't mean you can't or won't get a sizeable down payment, nor does it mean you have to keep this financing in place for 30 years. Over the years I have sold hundreds of houses using this method, and overall have had great success. I have also represented numerous sellers utilizing this strategy. Their goal was to create a reliable income stream. Many of the homes I financed, I kept the underlying bank financing in place, while receiving a down payment from the buyer. Normally I would require at least 5% down and in some cases received as much as $30,000 down! – Not much risk with a buyer putting that much money down. Why would buyers do this? Many times, the buyer can't qualify for traditional financing, and in our "post-crash" market, that is very often the case. If anyone has had so much as a "financial hiccup" on their record, not to mention a previous short sale, foreclosure, bankruptcy, or being self-employed they can pretty much write off the possibility of getting traditional bank financing for 1-3 years.

Most of the owner financing sales I originated, I would get a minimum of 5% down, and finance for a maximum of 1-2 years. Much like offering a lease purchase or "rent-to-own" I wanted to get my money out within a year or two. This provided a win-win for me as I would get some cash up front initially, and have monthly cash flow which would cover all of my monthly mortgage payment, taxes, insurance, etc....and hopefully an additional spread of cash flow. Offering these "special terms" allowed a much higher price to be negotiated. Obviously this price needs to be within reason, as the buyer will likely need to secure an appraisal at the time they "refinance' and secure new bank financing which in turn will pay you off.

Without getting into a lot of detail, this strategy can be used to eliminate any negative cash flowing properties and create a positive income stream. There are some minimal paper-work requirements when handling a contract for deed. This would include the initial contract, deed, disclosures, and providing annual 1098's to the buyers. It may initially sound complicated, but it's definitely not rocket science.

Chapter Nine – Closing The Deal!

This is what you've been planning and waiting for since you initially put your home on the market. If you've applied the ideas and strategies in this book, you've likely secured a fast, workable contract on your home for $5,000-$50,000 more than you would have without utilizing the information in this book.

If you're selling your home by owner, you'll need to secure a contract and forward a copy to the title company for them to process. Selecting a title company is an important task. It's a good idea to get referrals from others who have used them before. You can call around and negotiate fees to some degree, but better to spend an extra hundred bucks and have a dependable company that provides the service and reliability you would like. Over the years we've used numerous companies, and have found several that provide excellent service. We now primarily use one company that has proven themselves many times over the years and is also one of the highest rated title insurers in the Nation.

Hopefully by this time, all contract contingencies have been met. Some of them include:

- Building inspections
- Insurance
- Loan commitment

You've come a long way at this point, so don't let emotions run high, only to kill your deal right before it is scheduled to close. Over the past 20 years, I've only had a handful of situations where a deal almost fell apart on the day of closing due to either a buyer, seller or agent getting emotionally worked up for some reason or the other. Remember that the desired outcome is to sell your home. Don't ever lose sight of that outcome! One of the most important jobs I have as a real estate broker is to provide rational "non-emotional" advice to a client to ensure they make the absolute best decision possible in a particular transaction.

Another one of the most important jobs I have is to ensure absolutely everything up to this point has been handled efficiently, effectively, and nothing has been overlooked. As mentioned previously, I am an advocate of using checklists. As a pilot, I know without utilizing one, the chances you'll eventually forget something, which can lead to a mistake, accident or even a "crash" is greatly increased. In real estate, this equates to a missed deadline, contingency, contractual obligation, etc…This can mean losing thousands if not tens of thousands of dollars for myself or my client, or bring about costly litigation. Regardless of how or where you close, definitely make sure you have read and understand the contract and all time sensitive contingencies. Even missing a simple inspection contingency date can hold you liable for some costly repairs. Write down any and all contract deadlines and utilize a closing checklist. You'll ultimately be glad you did!

If you or your agent has followed my suggestions in this book, closings generally go pretty smooth. There are a few problems that can arise however which are usually out of your control. One is the buyers financing. Despite everyone doing everything correctly, and taking steps to ensure you close on time, there are times when the buyer's financing just doesn't happen as planned. There are numerous parties involved in the document acquisition phase and the financing decision for a buyer. You have the loan officer, appraiser, underwriter, PMI company, investor, insurance company, title company, employer, US Postal Service, IRS, etc…etc…One small snag in any of these numerous parties hands, and your closing gets delayed despite everyone's wishes. Lately, due to the large number of fraudulent IRS returns being filed, the IRS is backlogged and not providing timely tax transcripts to the lenders. This is just one of the many issues that can arise.

As of the publishing of this book, the TILA – RESPA Integrated Disclosure Rule that originated from the Dodd-Frank Wall Street Reform and Consumer Protection Act is soon scheduled to go into effect. It was originally scheduled for August and has now been put off until October. These new disclosure requirements were set up with the intent of protecting consumers. Despite their intent, they will definitely cause some headaches and delayed closing times if there is a loan involved with the purchase. One small change will ultimately cause the file to be re-disclosed and you can add a week on to your closing. Over the years, we have assembled an excellent group of lenders for almost every type of financing situation. Despite having lenders that I would literally trust with my life, they still occasionally run into a temporary snag with some area of a client's financing. Remember, a delay is not a denial! – Keep focusing on the end result and you will likely get there! Aside from financing issues, closings for the seller are pretty smooth. Not much to sign overall. Usually a closing statement, a few title company disclosures, and the warranty deed, and you're done. Basically, sign your name and collect your check...and hopefully if you've followed the directions in this book you'll collect an extra $5,000-$50,000 in the process!

Chapter Ten - The Many Advantages of Real Estate

Despite what many people think, real estate is one of the highest yielding investments with the overall lowest risk out there today! This may be a little difficult to accept, especially after just recovering from one of the largest downturns in the economy since the Great Depression. Now granted, if you purchased any real estate (at retail prices) at the peak of the market between 2006 and 2007 (at over-inflated prices,) and wanted to sell within the next 3-4 years, you would definitely argue this opinion with me! And, trust me! I got caught up in this dilemma too! Really bad! – Between 2006 and 2007, I was purchasing 3-4 houses per month to rehab and resell. I not only had lots of cash put into these multiple homes, but I had lots of mortgages too. At the end of 2007 I had a negative cash flow which included payroll, renovation costs, debt service coverage, and other incidentals in the range of $25,000 per month! Believe me! If anybody wanted to bad-mouth real estate, I definitely could, especially after living through the market crash! The only saving grace was that I only purchased homes and properties that were a least 20% below market. This did allow the sale of many of the homes before we lost a great deal of money from an "out of pocket" standpoint. However we still lost hundreds of thousands of dollars while paying the remaining mortgages, taxes and insurance until many of the properties sold.

As you may or may not know, what drives the market and economy is people's optimism or pessimism. That may seem overly simplistic, but ultimately that is the driving force. Throw in today's media, and we had the firestorm of market crash. Most people had a pretty good idea this would happen before it actually happened. I remember for several years prior to 2008, talking to people, and everyone saying: "Things are really great, but I wonder when the bubble will burst?" Over those two years, I would guess I heard that from at least several hundred people. That reality had already been created in everyone's mind. It was only a matter of time with the massive buildup of private debt, lenders lending too much, borrowers borrowing too much, bank regulations too loose, and the overall risk culture of the time that would lead to the cataclysmic downturn in the economy.

Regardless of this downturn, (which was second only to the Great Depression) if you had purchased like many people did in 2006-2007 (pre-crash) – even at retail prices, and held on during the next 5-6 years, you most likely got back all of the hypothetical "loss" you thought you incurred. As many investment advisors will tell you: You only "lost" money if you sold at that time. If this was a home you were living in, no loss incurred if you held on through the recovery period. If you bought in 2006-2007, got scared in 2008-2009 and decided to sell, well things probably didn't turn out to well for you! Also, if you were speculating or strictly investing with lots of leverage (debt service) during that time then you probably didn't fair to well either.

Despite the Great Depression and the Crash of 2008, real estate has still increased dramatically in value. Consider the cost of an average home in 1900: $1,500 In addition, most real estate can generate cash flow during the time it is being held. It can also be leveraged, if needed, and if purchased intelligently with and excellent exit strategy in place, it can provide enormous returns. In fact, during an up cycle, it requires very little knowledge whatsoever. An example: A friend of a friend of mine was purchasing lots in Florida during 2006. He was purchasing lots 100% leveraged with bank financing, holding them 3-6 months, and reselling them for a $10,000-$30,000 profit! – The friend of mine decided to do the same thing. He unfortunately didn't begin until the latter part of 2007. The market soon crashed and my friend basically lost the same amount of money per lot within the same amount of time. Timing is critical in real estate investing unless you are in it for the long haul!

Overall, during my real estate investing career, (1993-current) there have only been 3-4 years of true "market downturn" – Also, had I been a little more intelligent, listened to some of the signs, and not got side-tracked, I could have been set up to purchase properties at greatly reduced prices and made millions in a few short years. Many people did in fact, and are now reaping the rewards. My advice: Proceed with knowledge! Knowledge trumps caution, as with the proper knowledge you can make an educated decision which is intelligent and cautious in the areas needed.

Despite the crash, I look back at over 20 years of investing and can see many great returns. The first house I purchased was in 1993. It was a bank owned Fannie Mae property which I was able to purchase for $49,000. It was a 3 bedroom, 1.5 bathroom home with a two car tuck-under garage. (See picture on page 93)

First Investment Purchase in 1993 - Long-Term Rental
Initial Equity of $14,000 with $200 per month positive cash flow.

This home was in a great area but needed a good deal of work. Being my first investment purchase, I did many of the repairs myself. I spent a total of $7,000 (Not including sweat equity) on the home. New to investing, and low on funds, I purchased this house with funds from cash advances utilizing my credit cards. This would not normally the best way to go about buying a house, but it did allow me to pay cash, close quickly, and ultimately get a pretty good deal. Within 60 days I had the house ready to rent. I put a tenant in the property for $650 per month and immediately refinanced the property, promptly paying off all my credit cards.

Overall, the interest I paid on the cash advances was less than I would have spent putting some sort of traditional financing on the property, which would have been difficult due to the condition of the home. When the transaction was all complete, I had a property worth $70,000 with a total expenditure of $56,000 (20% equity) with a $200 per month positive cash flow...The following year, the house was worth around $75,000.....by 2007 the property was worth around $175,000!

With that win under my belt, I proceeded to purchase at least one house every few month for the first year. As business grew, I increased my purchases to at least one house per week for the next several years. Some of these houses we kept for long term rentals, some we quickly re-sold for a profit. Many of the homes we bought, we rehabbed, refinanced, and put them n the market as lease options/rent-to-owns or owner financed properties. During market "slow-downs" I offered this creative financing which allowed us to sell our inventory quickly when others were struggling.

Between the years 2000 and 2007, most of the homes we purchased were quickly "flipped" for an instant profit. The market was hot, and homes were appreciating rapidly. This allowed us a quick influx of cash to continue with additional projects. One of the homes we purchased in 2001 was a 100 year old brick home in the City of St. Charles. (See picture below) We acquired this home in April of 2001 for $94,000. We immediately began major renovation on the home. Within 3 months we had the home ready for sale with total renovation and holding costs just under $90,000. Within 30 days of completion and 90 days from our initial purchase we secured a contract for $284,000. This was our first $100,000 profit deal!

"Fix & Flip"
$100,000 Profit!

Another strategy that I would highly recommend is using self-directed IRA's for your investing portfolio. When I left my job at UPS, I had accumulated several hundred thousand dollars in a 401K. When I left UPS, I needed a new investment vehicle to allow this savings to grow. The self-directed IRA allowed me to purchase homes in the name of my IRA account, and sell them for a profit without incurring any taxable gain at that time. This investment strategy is available to anyone and most do not even know it exists. One of the first homes I purchase utilizing this strategy was in 1999. (see picture below…)

Self-Directed IRA "Double Closing"
$15,000 Net Profit within 30 days. (Tax deferred!)

I had placed a bid in for this property which was owned by the local fire department. It was a nice 3 bedroom, 1 bathroom house with a detached 4 car garage. I had offered $70,000 and was soon awarded the bid. The earnest money check for $500 was issued from my self-directed IRA account. Once the contract was accepted, I was given 30 days to close. During this time, I found a buyer who wanted the property for his business. I had originally planned on purchasing this property with funds from my self-directed IRA, but this new buyer was willing to pay $85,000 for the property. I went ahead and accepted his offer. Within 3 weeks we were completing a double closing on the property....This involved us both showing up at the title company. I signed my name, he signed his, and I collected $15,000. I literally did nothing else, and actually had never even seen the inside of this home. Actually this $15,000 profit went directly back into my IRA account (tax deferred!) When was the last time you invested $500 and made $15,000 in 30 days? That's a 3,000% return in 30 days......36,000% annual return! (Not to mention tax deferred and back in my IRA account ready to do another deal!) – As you can see this can be an extremely powerful investment strategy if used intelligently. This strategy offers very little risk - $500 in this case, with a great upside - $15,000 profit. Even if I had not found this buyer, I had planned on purchasing the home, fixing it up some and either renting it out or reselling it. The probability I would have made even more on the house was likely, and even if the market crashed, or something else happened not allowing me to purchase this property, the most I had at risk was my original $500 earnest money. In my opinion, this investment vehicle should be utilized by anyone wanting to increase their investment portfolio geometrically with very little risk! If anyone has additional questions about how to set up one of these accounts, or the companies offering it, feel free to contact me by phone or E-Mail which is provided in the back of this book.

Always remember that effective negotiating can save or make you money in almost any circumstance in life. From buying a home, business, or almost any purchase. In summary though, getting a "great deal" on real estate revolves around knowing where to look. As someone told me, "fish where the fish are!" It's difficult to get a great deal on a property that the owner has little or no motivation to sell, or if they owe more on the home than what you are willing to pay. (Unless there is a potential for a short sale) You will better your chances significantly by searching out and finding properties where there is a definite motivational factor involved. Some of these factors can include bankruptcy, insolvency, divorce, death, foreclosure, short sale, etc…etc…Not to say you can't get a good or even great deal searching else-where, you just limit the statistical chances significantly. Since one of the first steps in negotiations, is gathering information, you will likely have already found out the reason the seller is selling.

Since a distressed situation obviously provides more opportunity for securing a below-market purchase, this is where I would begin my search. When I first began investing in real estate, I contacted all of the banks and lending institutions to let them know of my new business of buying homes. Unfortunately, I spent a great deal of time talking to bankers with little response. Later in my career, I began developing relationships with several bank presidents and vice presidents. This in turn led to them contacting me as a prospective buyer. Ultimately, the relationship was what created the opportunity here, not just showing up promoting yourself as the banks savior. Developing a relationship, utilizing their services, opening an account, etc…all helped much more in securing their trust and ultimate cooperation. I have since either purchased or found hundreds of below-market properties for clients thanks to my personal contacts I've made over the years. Ultimately, being the expert in the field of buying distressed properties brings you a lot of business in itself. I receive calls daily from both buyers and sellers due to my long history of being in this business. If you do not have a long history, utilize someone who does. Finding a buyer's broker who specializes in acquisitions, negotiations, and buying below-market real estate can save you countless hours of time. Once you find someone like that, treat them well, and they will treat you well. When I first started out in the business, I found someone that specialized in these types of homes. I knew enough at this point to develop a relationship first, and to prove myself as a buyer. If I said I would purchase it, you could guarantee with 100% certainty I would perform on time, every time. After completing a handful of purchases and had adequately proved myself, I was now given priority as a buyer. I would be the first one called, and many times bought properties significantly below-market before any other investors even knew they were available. Occasionally I would even buy some properties with only a small amount of profit margin to secure my position as the "best buyer client" out there. I figured I was willing to forgo a larger profit margin on some, knowing I would be able to make up the difference on others I would likely get.

To sum-up this last chapter... Real estate can be one of the most powerful, wealth building vehicles on the planet if you educate yourself properly and as Nike® says: "Just Do It!"®

Chapter Eleven – Ensuring You Absolutely, Positively Sell Your House FAST and Make an Extra $5,000-$50,000!

On a road-trip back from Atlanta, my wife received a phone call from one of her sellers saying they were going to re-list their home with another individual and company. She had the home listed for almost (3) months, and the listing was scheduled to expire. This seller just happened to be the mother of a good friend, and my wife took this very hard, and was truly hurt that they would use someone else to sell their home.

Prior to listing this home, my wife had pulled all active, pending, expired, and sold comparable homes in the neighborhood and shared all of this data with the seller. Based on the homes recently sold, the ones currently active, and the condition of the home dictated a <u>list</u> price of somewhere between $185,000 and $193,500. The home was structurally sound, well taken care of, but very outdated. My wife shared all of this information with the seller and her family. This seller had lived in the home for the past 50+ years, raised a family there and for obvious reasons, was very emotionally attached. She had already purchased another home that was more size appropriate, so now owned two homes. Despite my wife's repeated price recommendation, the seller wanted the home to be listed for $215,000! – This was $25,000-$30,000 <u>more</u> than the home should be listed for! My wife again shared the information on the other homes that had sold and that were active on the market. Despite this, the seller still wanted the home to be listed for $215,000. So, ultimately my wife gave in, and listed the home for the price they requested. She was trying to be respectful of her friend's mother, and her wishes. She was also trying to be nice. Well, as you can probably guess.....She not only wasted her time, but also the time of the seller, and eventually created an uncomfortable situation for everyone involved. The bottom line here as we later discussed in the car.....This was not completely the sellers fault! No one <u>made</u> my wife list this home for $25,000-$30,000 more than it should be listed for. Granted, her intent was good, and she was trying to be respectful of her sellers, but the ultimate responsibility when it came to marketing and selling the home was up to my wife. As we discussed on the ride home, as agents we need to do whatever it takes to either convince the seller how it would be detrimental to their ultimate goal to sell the house or as a last resort recommend she list with someone else! Harsh words maybe, and definitely difficult when you're dealing with family and friends, but a valuable lesson learned. I have been guilty of this too! Earlier in my career, I had this happen on numerous occasions. – I now tell my sellers: Do you want me to tell you what you <u>want</u> to hear? Or, do you want me to tell you what you <u>need</u> to hear in order to sell your home fast and net more money?

In this scenario, my wife's client wanted to hear that their beloved (yet outdated and now overpriced) home was indeed worth $215,000. Unfortunately, that is not what she really <u>needed</u> to hear. She needed to hear and understand, and hear over and over again if need-be that by listing her house $35,000 over what it was worth would only hurt her in the long run. My wife would have had a much better chance of selling her home for $180,000 by listing it at $150,000 then $215,000! Had she listed it initially when the interest was highest "below market" at $150,000, she would have gotten a huge response and likely multiple offers and ultimately an offer of at least what the home was truly worth. I pulled this home up after is eventually sold and saw that the sold price was $173,500. With insurance and taxes, the seller likely had an extra $2,500 in holding costs, paid an extra $1,000 in commission and got less than they would had they listed for a correct price in the beginning. Truthfully, they very likely could have gotten an extra few thousand dollars <u>above</u> $180,000 had they listed at the appropriate price Ultimately pricing the home too high in this case cost them at least $10,000!

Irrational emotions, greed, or ignorance can cost you thousands of dollars when buying or selling a home. Put yourself in the shoes of a buyer....Would you purchase a home for $35,000 more than a comparable home just because the seller would like to get that price? Likely not! That goes for the majority of buyers these days. People have access to a huge amount of information and data online. You can instantly see what other homes are listed for and what has sold by utilizing Zillow, Trulia, Realtor.com, the tax records, etc...

I tell people every day: Even if I could magically make a buyer write a contract for $25,000-$35,000 more than a home is worth, the most likely scenario down the line would be the whole deal falling apart after the buyer's appraiser determines the value is less than the purchase contract.

Over the years, I have kept very good records, analyzed statistics, and recorded my results vs other agents in my market. I know with 100% certainty that when I list a home, and utilize our cutting edge marketing plan combined with the negotiation skills I have learned over the years, I can net my clients between 1.6% and 3.4% more than another agent in my market. The average home in St. Charles County is slightly over $200,000. This equates to a savings between $3,200 and $6,800 not including the additional savings from a reduced time on the market and the associated costs of insurance, taxes, and any mortgage payments. – This may not seem like a lot, but based on our goals of selling 200+ houses for the year, it ultimately saves my clients well over a million dollars. These statistics even take into account some of the past homes I have listed for friends and family at unrealistic prices much like my wife's recent experience. To offset pointing fingers at her, I'll share one of my past experiences:

Several years ago I had a friend whose husband had recently passed away. Before he died, he told his wife "Don't give the house away." After his passing, which was obviously an extremely emotional time for her, she had me list her home. Since her husband had told her not to give the house away, she had me list the home for well over $300,000. I provided her with all the comparable homes much like my wife did. This home was also priced around $30,000 over what the market would bear. I marketed this home heavily and did have a few lookers. A year went by however without a single offer. I again provided a new list of sold homes and active listings in their area which again showed that they were significantly overpriced. In an attempt to honor her wishes and her deceased husband, I did exactly what my wife did. In this case, I should have just told my friend that by listing her house at that price I would be doing a disservice to her and her family, and that I could not do that to her or anyone else….Sometimes it takes some backbone to not take a listing. Unfortunately there are numerous agents out there that prey on people's lack of knowledge and would be glad to tell them what they'd like to hear and then after listing the home for an inflated price, work them down to a price that would sell, while ultimately netting the seller even less due to the excessive time on the market and reduced interest.

Much like my wife's listing, the seller contacted me after a year and a half saying she would like to try a new agent (someone part-time with little experience) – Much like a football coach….a few losing seasons, and out with the coach. I had pulled up the listing almost two years later and the house was still listed for sale despite a 10% increase in property values during that time….go figure! – I'm sure the seller's deceased husband would not have wanted his wife to endure the stress and suffering of sitting on this house for several years. I realize most real estate agents have this happen during their careers, but in the car that day, I made a pact with my wife to never let this happen again! – By listing someone's house at an unrealistic price is not helping them in any way whatsoever! If you remember nothing from this book….remember…..DO YOUR

HOMEWORK! Look at what has sold in your neighborhood. (Compare similar type construction....ranches, two-stories, split levels, etc...) See what has sold in the past 90 days! Also look at what is currently listed in your neighborhood! See what your competition is! Take into account the condition of the home! If your house is terribly outdated, make adjustments! – BE SMART! – Even if you use an agent or broker that you trust, look at the information they provide! – Don't follow blindly! – Not doing this can cost you thousands if not tens of thousands of dollars!

Chapter Twelve – The Bottom Line

The last chapter of this book is inspired by the many of books I've read in my lifetime, and the many I continue to read. Almost every book I read, I gain valuable insights, ideas, thoughts, strategies, and useful techniques. Unfortunately, due to "sensory overload" and my inherent short term memory loss, I quite often forget the majority of what I just read!

When reading a new book, I often find myself underlining, highlighting, circling, and completely marking up the book in attempt to gather and store valuable information. (A good sign the book is worth reading!) I often then find myself taking additional notes in an attempt to highlight the idea and put it in a useful format for future use. This not only takes quite a bit of time, creates and abundance of notes and other files, but makes a mess of my books. (Not a good idea if they are borrowed books from the local library!)

Most individuals have a limited capacity when it comes to remembering or focusing on something. After a few ideas, most information gets lost in the "brain shuffle" A classic example of this is comes into play with my lovely wife Sallie. Many times during our relationship, she has approached me with a very "elaborate" story in an attempt to convey some obviously important information. As the story continues, she quite often notices my eyes wondering and an uncomfortable look on my face followed by some uncontrollable body "twitching" My wife quite often mistakes these bodily queues as a complete and utter disdain for her feelings, ideas, thoughts, and obvious eloquent use of the English language.

This could not be further from the truth! These bodily abnormalities occur due to my limited male attention span, and the mental overload I quite often feel. I tell my wife all the time: "There's a lot going on up here!" (Pointing to my large forehead) – How can she reasonably expect me to take in all of this information?

Truthfully, the way my mind works (or fails to work in most cases) is during a conversation, I ask myself the following question:

"What is the "One Thing" aka "Bottom Line" I need to know or do in order to successfully handle whatever "situation" is occurring?" – To me this just seems to be the logical way to efficiently "get things done." To all the men out there, please be careful however when you feel the inherent need to interrupt your loving spouses eloquent rendition of a story with the repeated question:

"Bottom Line?" "Bottom Line?" - I speak from experience here! On that note, please enjoy the following "Bottom Lines" from the book!

Chapter One

Bottom Line:
You absolutely, positively can sell your home extremely fast and make an extra $5,000-$50,000 if you follow the directions in this book!

Chapter Two

Bottom Line:
Do Your Homework! – Educate yourself on the following:
- Your property
- Your competition (other homes)
- The market
- Contractors & pricing
- Tax implications

Chapter Three

Bottom Line:
Make sure you prepare your home adequately prior to
putting it on the market. Utilize the checklist in the book
as a guide.

Bottom Line:
Do the math prior to completing any remodeling
projects to ensure you will <u>make</u> money.

Bottom Line:
Consider getting an ASHI certified home inspection
prior to putting your home on the market.

Chapter Four

Bottom Line:
Ensure you absolutely, positively utilize the services of
a marketing and negotiations specialist when selling
your home!

Chapter Five

Bottom Line:
Regardless of how you sell your home, make sure it is marketed "Massively"!

Chapter Six

Bottom Line:
Regardless of how you sell your home, make sure negotiations are handled professionally and effectively by:

- Gather all information (know everything!)
- Determine your options
- Develop a negotiation strategy.
- Be nice!

Chapter Seven

Bottom Line:
If needed or required during a slow-market utilize a "Lease Purchase" to eliminate the negative cash-flow and increase your chances of making or saving money on the transaction.

Chapter Eight

Bottom Line:
Consider utilizing "Owner Financing" to eliminate the negative cash-flow and increase your chances of making or saving money on the transaction.

Chapter Nine

Bottom Line:
Don't screw up the final closing due to high emotions!

Bottom Line:
Utilize a professional sales person who utilizes a checklist to avoid "crashes"!

Bottom Line:
Be patient! – A delay does not mean a denial!

Chapter Ten

Bottom Line:
Real estate can be one of the most lucrative investments on the planet if you do your home homework in advance and utilize the strategies in this book when selling!

Chapter Eleven

Bottom Line:
Do your homework and price your home intelligently! –
Don't over-price!

Chapter Twelve

Bottom Line:
The author of this book (yours truly) is far from a
marital expert! – Treat any advice in the beginning of
this last chapter cautiously!

Other Resources

For additional information please check out our website:

www.AmericanLandmarkRealty.com
- *Online Property Search*
- *FREE List of Pre-Foreclosures, Foreclosures & Short Sales!*
- *FREE Home Evaluation!*
- *FREE List of Home Prices in Your Area!*
- *Learn How to Sell Your Home Even if You Owe More Than It's Worth!*
- *Learn How to Make 50%+ Returns with Your IRA or Other Retirement Accounts!*
- *And Much More.....*

...or to contact me directly, please call:
314-956-6292

...or E-Mail me at:
Investing@Charter.net

We currently offer brokerage services in the state of Missouri and specialize in assisting buyers and sellers in maximizing their returns both on purchases and sales. We also offer one-on-one real estate investment consulting and a cutting edge VIP monthly mentoring program.

119

We also have several other books available:

30 MINUTE GUIDE TO NEGOTIATING LIKE A CHAMPION!

HOW TO MAKE OR SAVE $$ BIG MONEY $$ IN ALL YOUR NEGOTIATIONS!

#1 AUTHORITY ON REAL-ESTATE NEGOTIATIONS

STEVEN J. FELDEWERT

Quotes

"Every adversity, every failure, every heartache carries with it the seed of an equal or greater benefit."
-Napolean Hill

"You miss 100% of the shots you never take."
-Wayne Gretzky

"Be careful what you think about because you will surely get it."
-Thomas Carlisle

"Whether you think you can or think you can't, you're right."

-Henry Ford

"It doesn't matter where you start. It matters where you finish."
-Joe Martin

"Things turn out best for those who make the best of the way things turn out."
-John Wooden

"Success seems to be largely a matter of hanging on after others have let go."
-William Feather

"Don't let what you cannot do interfere with what you can do."
-John Wooden

"If you don't know where you are going, how can you expect to get there?"
-Basil S. Walsh

"Success is how high you bounce after you hit bottom."
-General George S. Patton

"Do what you do so well and so uniquely that your customers can't help but tell others about you."
-Walt Disney

"If you don't ask then you won't get. But if you will simply ask for what you want, then you will be amazed at what you will get."
-James Malinchak

"All things are difficult before they are easy!"
-Thomas Fuller

"Remember: It takes teamwork to make your dream work!"
-James Malinchak

"You can make more friends in two months by becoming interested in other people, than you can in two years by trying to get people interested in you."
-Dale Carnegie

"A goal is a dream with a deadline."
-Napoleon Hill

"Most "impossible" goals can be met simply by breaking them down into bite size chunks, writing them down, believing them, and then going full speed ahead as if they were routine."
-Don Lancaster

"Your goal should be just out of reach, but not out of sight."
-Denis Waitley & Remi Witt

"We are all faced with a series of great opportunities – brilliantly disguised as insurmountable problems."
-Johyn Gardner

"The difference between a successful person and others is not a lack of strength, not a lack of knowledge, but rather a lack of will."
-Vince Lombardi

"Only those who dare to fail greatly can ever achieve greatly."
-John F. Kennedy

"Failure is just another way to learn how to do something right."
-Marian Wright Edelman

"Failure is a trickster with a keen sense of irony and cunning. It takes great delight in tripping one when success is almost within reach."
-Napoleon Hill

"The only people who never fail are those who never try."
-Ilka Chase

"That which does not kill you makes you stronger."
-Neitzsche

Notes

Notes

Notes

Notes

Notes

Notes

Notes

Notes

Notes

Notes

Notes

Notes

www.ingramcontent.com/pod-product-compliance
Lightning Source LLC
Chambersburg PA
CBHW051314170526
45166CB00002B/538